THEOLOGY and SPIRITUALITY

Andrew Louth

SLG Press
Convent of the Incarnation
Fairacres   Oxford
OX4 1TB

Revised 1978
Fourth Impression 1994

ISBN 0 7283 0079 6
ISSN 0307-1405

Printed by Will Print, Oxford, England

This paper was first read to the Origen Society
on 30 October 1974

ACKNOWLEDGEMENT

The cover picture is taken from *The Mosaics of Monreale*
(plate 90, Cherubim), and is reproduced by kind permission
of the publishers, S. F. Flaccovio of Palermo

I

IN THE ACCOUNT of the trial of Jesus in the Fourth Gospel, Pilate brings his first examination to a close with the question, 'What is truth?' And the evangelist records that with this question Pilate turned away from Jesus. The *dramatic* significance of this is not much remarked on by the commentators, but it seems to me worthy of note. Pilate's question is not being asked seriously but is dismissive, for as he asks it he turns away from the man who can answer it. The dialogue with Jesus is at an end. Pilate has no wish to go any further with the acquaintance. It seems to me that here, as often, St John is suggesting that what we would normally regard as an intellectual inquiry—the pursuit of truth—and what we would not primarily regard as an intellectual matter at all—the development of a human relationship—are closely related and deeply interwoven. What I have to say in this paper is little more than comment on this suggestion of the fourth evangelist.

Let me begin by trying to explain what I understand theology to be. It is, as the word suggests, some sort of understanding of God, some sort of articulation of awareness of God, of his relation to the world, of his activity within the world. But who is this God? Such a question immediately poses a problem. Any easy answer to it would be no answer at all. For whatever else we think we know about God, ideas of his transcendence, his ineffability, and his mysteriousness, are ideas we cannot do without. Theology can go forward either by evading this question or living with it. Let me indicate some of the methods of evasion. We might proceed by saying: let us forget about the question as to who God is and simply look at what other people have said about God. Let us deal with *their* concepts. This way lies historical theology and the religious aspect of the history of ideas. Men *have* used the concept or category of God, let us see what they have to say about it. Such a study is serious and demanding, and passes the time wonderfully.

Another thing we might do—a rather more philosophical approach— is to elide the question, Who is this God? into a deceptively similar one, What is God? or, What is the divine? That we can get to work on, for we can discuss such an abstract, general question without raising the question as to whether there is, in fact, any such being as God at all. We discover in various forms a notion of the beyond in human experience. We discuss whether human existence can be understood without some concept of the transcendent. We know that men and societies are not self-sufficient, and we concentrate on those aspects of man's experience where any attempt at self-sufficiency is least plausible. Here, we say, we discover a religious dimension. We may go further and say that such a religious dimension cannot be in vain: there must be a God. And we perhaps think when we have got thus far that we have answered the question, Who is this God?

A familiar analogy suggests itself here. Who, we ask, is Professor X? We discover that he is involved in various areas of possible experience. He is head of such-and-such a department, editor of such-and-such a journal, author of a number of specific books and articles, married to Y, interested in, let us say, railways, and so on. We may in this way find out a great deal about him; we may in some way know who he is. But not in the way that his wife or a friend could be said to know him. They know *him*; we only know about him. We rather know what he is (various facts about him); they, who he is. Without meeting a person, speaking to a person, being introduced to a person, and yet knowing something about him, we might equally well say we 'know' him, or that we do not know him.

There is another similar analogy that might also be introduced here which is the analogy of the aesthetic experience. Aesthetic experience depends on the unique, though repeatable, experience of a work of art. One can say a great deal about a painting, a sculpture, a piece of music, a poem (the poem is slightly different in being verbal—the medium I use to speak about it); but one can only begin to know a work of art by experiencing it. We must expose ourselves to its uniqueness: communicable information about it will never enable us to work up the aesthetic experience in ourselves. The information about it is not irrelevant to the aesthetic experience—far from it. Such information can greatly increase our capacity to respond to art. But it plays a very different role in the experience itself than it would apart from the experience altogether.

Here then, we have two forms of experiencing—knowing a person, appreciating a work of art—that depend on something being *given* to us in experience: the person in his concrete actuality, the particular work of art. Now what I want to suggest is that something very like this is true of theology itself. The various forms of evading the question, Who is this God? are various ways of evading theology itself. Theology involves not a setting aside of the question, Who is this God? but a relentless attempt to answer it. Because of the nature of God, the answer to this question will be different from being introduced to a person, or from standing in front of a picture, because nothing in our experience can encompass the reality that God is. It will, however, be more like being introduced to a person, or standing in front of a picture, than the evasions of historical theology, or natural theology, or theological anthropology.

It is here that we can say, and must say, 'and spirituality', for spirituality, as I understand it, is about the apprehension of the reality of God. Spirituality is about prayer; and it is in prayer that the question, Who is this God? is answered. What do I mean by prayer? Not 'saying prayers'. For

> ... prayer is more
> Than an order of words, the conscious occupation
> Of the praying mind, or the sound of the voice praying.[1]

By prayer I understand something like waiting on God, openness to God of the whole person in stillness. That is easily said, but much less easily done—which is why, I imagine, there are so many books on prayer, some of them quite long. Spirituality, then, is about preparing a person to wait on God in stillness. There is discussion of methods of meditation or contemplation, ways of preparing to enter into stillness. There are descriptions and discussions of the experience of prayer, for others have gone that way before and we may learn from them. But the keynote is waiting and openness. For one thing is crystal clear in all the mystics and spiritual writers: that we are preparing for an experience we cannot evoke. Contemplation, awareness of God, is something given; for the God of whom we come to be aware is not a passive and impersonal ground of the universe, but a living and personal God who discloses himself to us. 'We could not allow the name of God to a being on whose privacy an Actaeon could intrude, or whose secrets a Prometheus could snatch from him without his assent', said C. C. J. Webb in one of his books.[2] The truth of that is presupposed in the writings of the mystics. Their God is not a God whom we discover but a God who reveals himself, a God who comes.

So spirituality—prayer—is, I suggest, that which keeps theology to its proper vocation, that which prevents theology from evading its own real object. Spirituality does not exactly answer the question, Who is God? but it preserves the orientation, the perspective, within which this question remains a question that is being asked rather than a question that is being evaded or elided.

I want to go a little further than this. But even having gone thus far there is a host of questions we must look at. Spirituality is necessary to theology to keep it in its proper vocation. The converse also seems to me true, that theology is necessary to spirituality to keep *it* to *its* proper vocation. 'He who prays is a theologian; a theologian is one who prays', to quote Evagrius. The danger of a non- or un-theological spirituality is, I think, that it will tend to become a mere cult of devotion, or devotedness, not to anything in particular but just in itself.

Now there is nothing new or unusual in such a view of the interdependence of theology and spirituality. It was, after all, the case with patristic theology, and has not been unknown since. Thomas Merton, the Trappist monk, had this to say:

> Contemplation, far from being opposed to theology, is in fact the normal perfection of theology. We must not separate intellectual study of divinely revealed truth and contemplative experience of that truth as if they could never have anything to do with one another. On the contrary, they are simply two aspects of the same thing. Dogmatic and mystical theology, or theology and 'spirituality', are not to be set apart in mutually exclusive categories, as if mysticism were for saintly women and theological study were for practical but, alas, unsaintly men. This fallacious division perhaps explains much that is actually lacking both in theology and spirituality. But the two belong together. Unless they are united there is no fervour, no life and no spiritual value in theology, no substance, no meaning and no sure orientation in the contemplative life.[3]

It would be possible, I suppose, to go on now and show how this interdependence between theology and spirituality is broadly maintained in patristic theology (and we will dip into Diadochus of Photicé later on), and is still the case with Anselm, the Victorines and others,

4

but how by the time of the Renaissance there had appeared a divorce between them: Thomas à Kempis's *Imitation of Christ* is hardly a work of theology but a work of devotion, and Cajetan's little treatise on analogy, say, is scarcely a work of spirituality. The history might be continued and we might discuss how various more recent theologians have attempted to bridge the gulf they have recognized and deplored between theology and spirituality. However, such an attempt is quite beyond me. What I shall do is to try and see this interdependence of theology from various angles in the hope that it may become clearer, and also attempt to relate what I say to what we actually find theology to be, as studied at the present time.

II

To take up the point with which I began this paper, let us consider the question of truth in theology. There seem to me to be broadly two tendencies within theology. One is closely related to some notion of propositional truth: the doctrines of Christianity make various assertions that we can check against the facts. This can take very diverse forms. A conventionally orthodox form uses such a notion of truth and tests the truth of theological statements by referring back to some guaranteed set of propositions, the Bible, say, or the Councils. An extreme form of this is the brand of Roman Catholic theology that Karl Rahner has called 'Denzinger-theology'.[4] Denzinger is a very useful volume which gathers together conciliar and papal utterances on most theological topics. To do Denzinger theology you look up your doctrine in the extremely comprehensive index and piece together all the extracts to which it refers. The logic of such a theology is that Denzinger consists of a collection of true theological statements with reference to which any theological utterance may be checked. This is an extreme form of the use of some notion of primarily propositional truth in theology. It can take many forms; it can even attempt to dispense with criteria. But its characteristic is a search for propositions that enshrine the truth. Apart from the objective criteria—Scripture, creeds, Denzinger, or whatever—the appeal is to reason, or, I would prefer to say, to *discursive* reason.

The other tendency in theology rejects such notions as propositional truth. The criterion here is what one might call *authenticity*. What is important is the authenticity of a certain attitude to life. A great deal is made of the fact that the articulation of our deepest concerns is difficult and halting. Revelation is not of propositional truth but of truth in a person, Jesus Christ: theological truth is found in the authenticity discovered in our response to that person. This tendency can, of course, take forms less orthodox.

Both these tendencies in the understanding of truth seem to me to have points in their favour. With the first it is at least clear that we are concerned with truth in some recognizable sense: there is, for instance, the possibility of error, and some means of detecting it. The second tendency is surely right in its insistence that something as deeply true as theology must be, if it is to be worth anything, will not be easy of access and therefore the object of much groping, and also in its awareness that acceptance of God's revelation is more than a merely intellectual matter.

At the beginning of his *The Mystical Element of Religion* Baron von Hügel draws attention to the 'apparent interior antimony' that exists between 'the particular concrete experience that alone moves us and helps us to determine our will but which, seemingly, is untransferable, indeed unrepeatable; and the general abstract reasoning which *is* repeatable, indeed transferable, but which does not move us or help directly to determine the will'. Von Hügel's 'apparent interior antimony' seems to me closely analogous to the two tendencies in the understanding of truth that I have suggested we can find in theology. He sees the antimony resolved in the saintly life. I do not want to pursue that here but rather revert to my earlier analogies of knowledge of a person and aesthetic experience. For in both these experiences there is a similar antinomy between what is communicable but inadequate, and what is incommunicable but which we feel to be the core, the essence of the experience, what the experience really is. If then, as I was saying earlier, you ask me of someone I know but you have never met, 'What is he like?' I may be able to tell you a great deal, but in the end I have to say, 'Well, you'll see what I mean if you meet him.' Similarly with a picture or a piece of music, I can communicate something, by comparison with things that you do know, by trying to evoke in you what it evokes in me. But all such attempts are notoriously uncertain. If you really want to know you must meet the person, see the picture, listen to the piece of music.

Something like this seems to me to be true of theology. There is a great deal that is to be said, a great deal that is communicable, but the core of the matter is something you must apprehend for yourself. Theology is neither concerned exclusively with the truth of certain doctrines, nor with the validity of a certain way of life, but with the response of loving devotion to the revelation of God's love and God's glory in Jesus Christ—a response that involves an orientation of our whole being, a way of life, and the articulation of that glory in what we call doctrine. 'Contemplation', says Richard of St Victor, 'is a free and clear vision of the mind fixed upon the manifestation of wisdom in suspended wonder.' It is in *contemplation* that theology and spirituality meet. Theology is one of the fruits of contemplation, the attempt to express and articulate what is perceived in this 'free and clear vision'; spirituality is the preparing of the soul for contemplation. And contemplation, in this sense, is not something we can attain. In technical language (no longer favoured but still quite useful), it is not acquired but infused contemplation, our responding to God's loving gaze, a gaze which in some way is centred on, concentrated in, the life and death of Jesus of Nazareth.

This may all sound very fine. But how, you might ask, does it relate to what we study as theology in this university, to study of the Old and New Testaments, to study of the history of doctrine, to study of doctrine itself, philosophy of religion, church history, and so on?

Both my analogies—knowledge of a person, aesthetic experience—in some way coincide in the experience of *loving* a person. For, to the lover, the beloved is apprehended not only as a person, but as being beautiful. And this, the most intense and deep way of knowing a person, yields a heightened sense of the *uniqueness* of the beloved. Everything about the person loved is drawn into the apprehension of, and delight in, the beauty of the beloved. The response of the lover to his beloved pervades his whole life in a way that unifies. The idea, say, that love imposes certain duties on the lover seems absurd, somewhat grotesque to the lover, for those duties are delights. He finds delight in everything about the beloved and does not tire of studying her in all her aspects. The lover can tell you a great deal about his beloved. Now it seems to me that orthodox Christianity offers the same possibility in relation to

7

the incarnation of God's love in the person of Jesus Christ. And the pursuits of academic theology are not unlike the fascination of the lover in all the aspects of his beloved. Let me explain . . .

III

Academic theology, as we know it, consists of a study of the Bible, study of the history of the Church and her teachings, and a systematic reflection on all that. It involves a whole variety of disciplines: linguistic, philosophical, and historical. The coherence of academic theology seems to me to depend upon the centrality of the person of Christ to theology. The New Testament comes within the compass of academic theology for it is the primary witness to the historical person, Jesus Christ, and to the response of those who knew him, the apostles—the nucleus, not just of the early Church, but of the Church as a whole. For the Church of the Resurrection is not limited to those alive at any one time but includes all who have responded to Christ. The Old Testament comes within the purview of academic theology (we are not Marcionites) essentially, it seems to me, because the God whom Jesus called Father is clearly the God of the Old Testament, not some abstract philosophical being. Christians have spoken of the Old Testament as the *prophetic* witness to Jesus. I do not think this need be—in fact I do not think it can be—understood in any naïve way, as if predictions of the prophets came true in Jesus. The prophetic witness—itself not isolated but seen in the context of the Old Testament people of God, its history, its institutions, and its reflections on the good life and God's dealings with men—the prophetic witness, in that sense, provides the matrix within which Jesus was able to speak of the Father. '*Ein Ausdruck hat nur im Strome des Lebens Bedeutung*—an expression has meaning only within the stream of life', said Wittgenstein. The words of Jesus likewise had meaning only within a stream of life and that life was the life of Israel. A search for *ipsissima verba Christi* in any sense which totally isolated them from their context would have no meaning. History of doctrine and ecclesiastical history have importance as clarifying and deepening our understanding of the 'stream of life' within

8

which *our* response to Christ has meaning. Philosophical and dogmatic theology is our attempt to articulate our understanding of what we believe, our exercise of *fides quaerens intellectum*.

Some sort of broad understanding of the coherence of academic theology seems to me to be necessary if we are to retain any idea of theology as a serious academic discipline. Now I know that many do not agree with that. Why not study the Old and New Testaments, history of the Church, history of doctrine, simply in themselves as purely academic subjects? Or, more strongly, must we not do so? I think those who say this do not understand what would be meant by taking this proposal seriously. If those branches of academic theology do not come within the ambit of a *fides quaerens intellectum*—faith seeking understanding—then I do not think they will stand together at all except as an arbitrary collection of diverse disciplines. Apart from presuppositions grounded in a view of theology as 'faith seeking under-standing', the Old Testament becomes a collection of Semitic writings, to be seen as part of a much larger group of Semitic and other near-eastern writings. You may say that is true, and ought to be recognized anyway. But with this difference: that the Old Testament scholar studies Ugaritic, or whatever, in order to throw light on the Old Testament. For apart from the presupposition implied in seeing study of the Old Testament as basic to Christian (or Jewish) theology, studying the Old Testament in order to throw light on Ugaritic texts comes equally within his purview. His specialization in the Old Testament is merely then of accidental significance, dictated simply by the finitude of the human mind, a specialization no more significant than that of the Anglo-Saxon scholar who specializes in *Beowulf*. Similarly, the New Testament becomes a group of Jewish and Hellenistic Jewish writings of the first century. Vermes has criticized New Testament scholars for studying Rabbinic material and the Dead Sea Scrolls simply as background to the New Testament. Unless we can accept the theological presupposition that sees study of the New Testament as part of Christian theology his criticism is surely justified and demands a total reorientation of New Testament scholarship. (Such a reorientation may be necessary anyway— but that is another matter.) Most of the early Church doctrine would thus become a mere strand—historically important because of Constantine—in the history of ideas of the later Roman Empire. Peter Brown's book, *The World of Late Antiquity*, provides a clear example

9

of the difference which results from this shift in perspective. And so on.

Academic theology, therefore, needs some understanding of its own inner coherence to justify itself at all as an academic discipline, otherwise the several disciplines of which it consists really themselves belong not together but to other wider disciplines. And such coherence is found, I have suggested, when the pursuits of academic theology are experienced as being not unlike the absorption of the lover in all the aspects of his beloved. Or perhaps that might be better put by saying the delight of the beloved in all the aspects of her lover. For Christ is revealed as the incarnation of God's love for us: *he* is the great lover, and the Church is his beloved, and we in her. Academic theology finds its coherence, literally comes into being as a possibility, as we find in Christ God loving us and longing for our love. And it is this response to God's love for us that is the central concern of spirituality. Prayer is *in essence* the loving pursuit of the beloved. The great part that *silence* plays in prayer has an analogy in the fact that silence becomes a mode of communion, and not an embarrassing pause, between people deeply devoted to one another. It is not without significance that the favourite single genre of mystical theology takes the form of commentary on the Song of Songs.

But how *academic* is this academic theology? I am quite sure that it is no less rigorous seen in this light than it is in any other context. And indeed the rigours of the perhaps apparently spiritually arid disciplines of academic theology have a positive and important significance for spirituality.

> *Wird Christus tausendmal zu Bethlehem geboren*
> *Und nicht in dir, du bleibst doch ewiglich verloren.*
>
> *Das Kreuz zu Golgotha kann dich nicht von dem Bösen,*
> *Wo es nicht auch in dir wird aufgericht', erlösen.*
>
> (Though Christ in Bethlehem a thousand times was born
> But not in thee, in all eternity thou art forlorn.
>
> The Cross in Golgotha, from evil never can,
> Unless thou rais'd it in thy heart, remit the ban.)[5]

So Angelus Silesius in his *Cherubinischer Wandersmann*. And in this he is echoed by many mystics and spiritual writers, particularly of the Rhineland school. And it is very true. But it is dangerous. For without any correcting influence the 'Christ born in me' will become the sort of Christ who *can* be born in me. He will tend to lose the historical lineaments of the first-century Jew he was. He will lose his strangeness. He will cease to be the one who confronts me in his sovereign individuality. Academic theology, the dispassionate study of the witness to Jesus of Nazareth, can provide that corrective. Sir Edwyn Hoskyns, the great Cambridge theologian, in the course of a discussion on the necessity of Greek in the theological tripos in that University—*plus ça change, plus c'est la même chose*—based his argument on the 'fact that the Gospels are strange to us men of the twentieth century and that to pass the gulf which separates us from them is an infinitely difficult task. "Now," says Hoskyns, "learning Greek is part of that task. The strange language is a symbol of the strangeness of thought that must be passed through before we can understand the Gospels aright." '[6]

In this light, academic theology can preserve the givenness, the prevenience, the reality of the Christ to whom we respond in love. It can limit a tendency for our Lord to be domesticated, to become one who is merely familiar, in the hearts of those who love him; and also a tendency for the prevenience of God's grace to become simply an abstract presupposition. God is not merely sovereign, but One who comes; *has* and *does* come. And what he was in Jesus—self-emptying love, defenceless, interpreting his sovereignty in an irrevocable love for men—that he really is. There is no more ultimate manifestation of God still to be learnt.

IV

THEOLOGY INTERPRETING SPIRITUALITY, and spirituality informing theology: that is the understanding of theology and spirituality I want to suggest to you. The theologian is one who prays, and one who thinks about the object of his loving prayer. It would therefore seem to me odd if he did not also think about his prayer. So, part of the formation of a theologian is the study of spirituality, not just as another branch of the history of doctrine, or whatever, but as a deepening of his own life of prayer. There are also academic—scholarly—issues involved here; different understandings of contemplation, say. How odd, then, if the theologian were not interested in these, primarily as a way to an intelligent understanding of his own prayer, and not as another specialization within theology. All this, you may say, presupposes that the theologian is a believer. It does—though not perhaps in such a heavily orthodox way as the question might seem to suggest. Certainly not an *unquestioning* believer. Newman saw theology as making progress by being 'alive to its own fundamental uncertainties'. But the theologian *must seek to be open to the object of his study*. That does not seem to me to be a very restrictive requirement. But I am saying that only some can really understand theology, only those who, in however slight a way, have begun to respond in love to God's love for them in Jesus Christ. And that has a parallel in an undoubted fact about human relationships, that one can only know another—or begin to know another—if towards that other there is something of the openness of love in one's attitude. 'Give me a lover, he will feel that of which I speak,' Augustine breaks out in his commentary on St John. 'Give me one who longs, who hungers, who is a thirsty pilgrim in this wilderness, sighing for the springs of his eternal homeland. Give me such a man; he will know what I mean.' (26.4.)

It might be felt that this attempt to draw theology (including academic theology) and spirituality so closely together founders from another point of view. I quoted Evagrius: the theologian is one who prays; one who prays is a theologian. Am I not making *prayer* an unduly, impossibly, academic and intellectual exercise? Surely prayer can—must—be an activity that can be practised by the simple and uneducated. And yet he who prays, says Evagrius, is a theologian. In an essay entitled 'Tradition and the Individual Talent' T. S. Eliot argued that for a poet to continue his vocation beyond his twenty-fifth year he needed to write 'with a feeling that the whole of literature of Europe from Homer, and within it the whole of the literature of his own country, has a simultaneous existence and composes a simultaneous order'. In the course of his essay, Eliot answers the objection (closely analogous to the objection to my thesis I have just raised) that such a conception of the poet makes the business of writing poetry an excessively intellectual affair:

> I am alive to a usual objection to what is clearly a part of my programme for the métier of poetry. The objection is that the doctrine requires a ridiculous erudition (pedantry), a claim which can be rejected by appeal to the lives of poets of any pantheon. It will even be affirmed that much learning deadens or perverts poetic sensibility. [A similar claim has often been made about the effect of academic theology on prayer.] While, however, we persist in believing that a poet ought to know as much as will not encroach upon his necessary receptivity and necessary laziness, it is not desirable to confine knowledge to whatever can be put into a useful shape for examinations, drawing rooms, or the still more pretentious modes of publicity. Some can absorb knowledge, the more tardy must sweat for it. Shakespeare acquired more essential history from Plutarch than most men could from the whole British Museum. What is to be insisted upon is that the poet must develop or procure the consciousness of the past and that he should continue to develop this consciousness throughout his career.[7]

Mutatis mutandis, I would want to say much the same about the bearing of theology on prayer. Some can absorb enough essential theology for their contemplation to have 'substance, meaning, and a sure orientation'[8] from the New Testament and the *Philokalia*, say. Others need a real immersion in the disciplines of theology. And further: both in our apprehension of our civilization, and in our response to God, we are not alone, we belong to one another. The artist does his work within a cultural context which he receives, and that may have been formed, at least in part, by less intuitive men than himself—by

13

those who must sweat for knowledge. Shakespeare belonged to the Renaissance, and the ideals of the Renaissance owe not a little to the scholars. There ought—there must be—some similar symbiosis between the contemplative and the theologian. More deeply so, for the tradition within which they work and pray is not merely the flux of men and events, but is influenced by the Spirit, the stream of that life which the Church, *qua* Church, lives.

V

We can learn something more about the relationship of the theologian and the contemplative from a fifth-century Greek bishop, Diadochus of Photicé. Apart from his writings, which were mystical in content and much used by Eastern monks, all we know about him is that he was a supporter of the Council of Chalcedon against the Monophysites. His main work is his *Century of Gnostic Chapters* on the spiritual life. There we read:

> The theologian whose soul is penetrated and enkindled by the very words of God advances, in time, into the regions of serenity (*apatheia*). For it is written: the words of the Lord are pure words, silver which has been purified in the fire from any taint of earth. The contemplative (*gnostikos*), strengthened by powerful experience, is raised above the passions. But the theologian tastes something of the experience of the contemplative, provided he is humble; and the contemplative will little by little know something of the power of speculation, if he keeps the discerning part of his soul free from error. But the two gifts are rarely found to the same degree in the same person, so that each may wonder at the other's abundance, and thus humility may increase in each, together with zeal for righteousness. For this reason the apostle says: For to one is given by the Spirit the word of wisdom, to another the word of knowledge by the same Spirit.[9]

For Diadochus, the theologian and the contemplative complement

14

one another. The contemplative (*gnostikos*) participates in knowledge (*gnosis*), the theologian in wisdom (*sophia*). The contemplative knows by experience, the theologian declares what is thus known. The theologian does not, however, interpret directly the experiences of the contemplative, rather he interprets Scripture, for the Scriptures witness to the mystery which the contemplative knows. 'Knowledge unites a man to God through experience, but without moving his soul to speak of these things . . . Knowledge comes by prayer, in great stillness and complete detachment; wisdom, by humble attention to the Scriptures and, above all, by the grace of God who gives it.' (Ch. 9.)

The theologian and the contemplative each share to some extent in the other's gift, but each has his own vocation. One might picture their relationship by thinking of a circle and its centre. The contemplative holds to the centre, the still centre, and knows (*gnosis*); the theologian carries the power of the centre outwards, manifesting it as wisdom (*sophia*). Neither the contemplative nor the theologian is separated from the other: there is something of the theologian in the contemplative, and of the contemplative in the theologian. Such an analogy, however, suggests a certain priority of the knowledge of the contemplative over the wisdom of the theologian and recalls Plotinus: 'When we look outside of that on which we depend we ignore our unity; looking outwards we see many faces. Look inward and all is the one head. If a man could but be turned about . . . he would see at once God and himself and the All.' (*Enneads* VI. 5. 7.)

For Plotinus contemplation is attachment to the centre. To look outwards, to move towards the circumference, and so be drawn into multiplicity and activity, is to fail in contemplation. Such a natural interpretation of the metaphor of the circle suggests that the theologian is a contemplative *manqué*; but to think thus is to misunderstand Diadochus. For him it is *theologia*, not *gnosis*, that is the 'first child of divine grace'. (Ch. 67.) Nothing, he says, kindles the heart to love of God so much as theology; through theology the soul enters the company of the ministering spirits, the angels.

The angelic life—that is the life the theologian leads, declaring the manifold wonders of God's glory to the faithful. In Diadochus' day the theologians were not professors but bishops who pursued their theology in the midst of the assembly of the faithful. This may seem a long way from what we have come to think of as theology. And yet not so far.

15

Most of the greatest Anglican theology has been produced by those who served the Church as bishops and pastors. Nor is such theology the pious edification one hears so often nowadays from the pulpit: it is an *exact* tracing of the glory of God. It is not insignificant that the one thing we know about Diadochus is that he was a supporter of the Chalcedonian definition against the Monophysites. He was not one who sat light to dogma, feeling that edification or mystical experience alone really mattered. For him the theologian traces the effulgence of God's glory, the contemplative holds to the still centre of that glory. Each needs the other, but the gift of the theologian, as Diadochus understands it, is the more precious. His thought here is echoed in some words of Hans Urs von Balthasar:

> For the rhythm of creation is not that it flows out from God in procession and then in a movement of return goes back whence it came. Rather both are one and undivided, the outgoing no less absolute than the return, the sending out no less God's will than the longing to return. Perhaps more divine than the homecoming to God is the going out from God, for this is the greatest thing, not that we should recognize God by flowing towards him, reflected like light from a mirror, but that we should proclaim him, like burning torches of light.[10]

VI

Finally, there seems to be another matter I must look at. Some might object to theology because it diverts Christians from their main concern which is to do God's will in the world. They might also object in a similar way to spirituality, and find in my paper an understanding of Christianity that is wholly introspective and irrelevant to the real concerns and needs of men. Jesus, they could say, was neither a theologian nor a mystic but a practical man who went about doing good. I have drawn together theology and spirituality by seeing them as both essentially *contemplative*. But, the argument against this runs, Christianity is not contemplative but active and practical. If theology has any place at all it is in thinking out how Christian action might be most fruitful, by analysing society, and so on. It is, on the contrary, essentially political and social.

I raise this because I profoundly disagree with such an interpretation of Christianity. Christianity certainly has an active side: the commandment to love is two-fold. But real action grows out of contemplation, the second commandment out of the first. Only in this way do we bring *God's* love to men. Indeed, doing good to other people is, in itself, an ambivalent activity; it can have many motives, some very suspect. 'She goes around doing good to people. You can tell who they are by their hunted look'—as the old joke puts it. Real concern for people is a fruit of contemplation: it involves a willingness to let them be themselves, to relinquish our efforts on their behalf, and to let them *be* in God. To quote Balthasar again: 'When we abandon our neighbour to God he continues to be supported by our love, and the pain of our being unable to help him accomplishes more than any self-confident action. That is why Thérèse of Lisieux regarded the contemplative Carmelite vocation as the most fruitful of apostolates.'[11] And in the treatise on the 'Four Degrees of Passionate Charity', the highest of Richard of St Victor's ascending degrees of love is concerned with our neighbour:

> In the first degree she [the soul] goes forth on her own behalf, in the last she goes forth because of her neighbour. In the first she enters in by meditation, in the second she ascends by contemplation, in the third she is led into jubilation, in the fourth she goes out by *compassion.*[12]

It is an element in the contemplative tradition we do well to remember. And it seems to me that theology is saved from a narcissistic irrelevance, not by a partial abandonment of theology, to devote the time saved to loving our neighbour; but by a deepening of the essential core of theology: contemplation. Contemplation makes theology possible. It is also the perfection of theology and, in that perfection, the soul 'goes out by compassion' and loves the other in God with a deeper love than any human well-wishing.

*　　*　　*　　*　　*　　*　　*　　*

NOTES

1. T. S. Eliot, 'Little Gidding' in *Four Quartets*, Faber and Faber, p. 36.

2. *Problems in the Relation of God and Man*, London 1911, p.25f.

3. *Seeds of Contemplation*, Anthony Clarke Books (paperback) 1972, pp.197-8.

4. Denzinger: *Enchiridion Symbolorum, Definitionum et Declarationum*, an invaluable collection of quotations from Councils and popes on dogmatic questions first compiled by Henry Denzinger in 1854 and since then revised by various people (including Rahner). The latest edition, edited by Adolf Schönmetzer, was published in 1976.

5. Quoted in *Love Alone: The Way of Revelation* by Hans Urs von Balthasar, London 1968, p.35.

6. Hoskyns, *Cambridge Sermons*, London 1938, p.xxiii.

7. T. S. Eliot, *Selected Essays*, Faber and Faber, pp.16f.

8. Cf. Thomas Merton, loc. cit.

9. Chapter 72. *Century of Gnostic Chapters* (an alternative translation might be *A Century on Contemplative Prayer*) can be found in: Diadoque de Photicé, *Oeuvres Spirituelles*, edited by E. des Places SJ, Sources Chrétiennes 5, third edition, Paris 1966.

10. *Das Herz der Welt*. Second, revised edition, Zürich 1944, p.19.

11. *Love Alone* ... (see n.5 above), p.94.

12. Richard of Saint-Victor, *Selected Writings on Contemplation*, translated by Clare Kirchberger, London 1957, p.224 (my italics).